PASTA

Project Manager
FRANCESCO DE CAROLIS
Editor and Photography Director
MELISA TEO
Designer
NELANI JINADASA
Production Manager
SIN KAM CHEONG
Editorial Assistant
INCI SARP

First published in 2002 by **Editions Didier Millet**
121 Telok Ayer Street, #03-01, Singapore 068590
Telephone: +65.6324 9260 • Facsimile: +65.6324 9261 • Website: www.edmbooks.com

For **Agnesi Asia Pacific**
B-503 Twin Building Daikanyama, 30-8 Sarugaku-cho Shibuya-ku Tokyo, 150-0033 Japan
Telephone: +81.3.5458 7601 • Facsimile: +81.3.5458 7602 • Website: www.colussigroup.it

And **Agnesi 1824 S.P.A**
Via T. Schiva 80, 18100 Imperia, Italy
Telephone: +39.0183.7031 • Facsimile: +39.0183.703 232 • Website: www.colussigroup.it

Silver flatware, holloware and crystal courtesy of Christofle (www.christofle.com)

Colour separation by Singapore Sang Choy
Printed in Singapore by Tien Wah Press (Pte) Ltd

© 2002 Editions Didier Millet
Photographs © Jörg Sundermann
Text © Don Bosco

COVER: **Sophie Chiarini enjoys a plate of freshly cooked Agnesi pasta.**

BACK COVER: **Spaghetti Chitarra with Green and White Asparagus Sauce (recipe on page 18).**

ISBN: 981-4068-51-9

PASTA

Chef
DIEGO CHIARINI
Author
DON BOSCO
Photographers
JÖRG SUNDERMANN
LAI CHOON HOW

CONTENTS

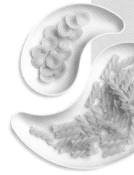

PASTA: THE LONG AND SHORT OF IT

Better Living Through Pasta

Promise a fine Italian meal and most people around the world today will immediately look forward to a delicious plate of pasta.

Historical sources indicate that it was actually the Chinese who first discovered the art of producing noodles as far back as 1,100 BC. Thanks to Italian adventurer Marco Polo's legendary visit to the East around the 13th century, his countrymen came to embrace this simple Oriental staple derived from cooking thin noodle strips sliced from a slab of dough.

Over the centuries since, the Italians have proudly established their own entirely unique culture around pasta, with hundreds of shapes and names, as well as types of sauces. Passionate debate still ensues over whether the Italians could have somehow invented such noodles, independent of Marco Polo's discovery. According to some, a set of 400 BC reliefs on an Etruscan tomb, illustrated with what looks like a pasta board, a pin, and equipment for shaping small pasta tubes, suggests a possibility.

Just as noodles symbolise longevity in the Far East, pasta in Italy is a national celebration of the people's famous passion for life. Italian culinary traditions are based on regional home cooking secrets that have been perfected and passed down over many generations. Even the bulk of recipes developed and guarded by today's top Italian chefs have been diligently reconstructed from this heritage. Italians also insist on top quality ingredients, using spices and sauces only to highlight the flavours of the main ingredient.

Finally, Italian cooking is shaped by its history and geography, which accounts for the mind-boggling diversity surrounding pasta. For centuries before the rise of modern communications, a good part of the land was filled with isolated valleys in which inhabitants developed their own cooking styles. Each region developed as a self-contained entity and their cuisine shows contrastive influences from

European culture up north, to the North African spice trade around the Mediterranean regions. The pasta industry sprang up around Sicily and Campania in the 18th century as durum wheat, commonly used to make pasta, grew particularly well in the climate there.

In all, these traits broadly account for the evolution of the rich and satisfying world of pasta today.

Shapes and Sizes

Fresh pasta (pasta fresca) is traditionally made with flour and eggs in North and Central Italy, and is perishable within a few days. Dry pasta (pasta secca), which has a much longer shelf life, originated from North and South Italy where durum wheat was widely available. As pasta machines were not yet introduced in the early days, the dry climates in these areas also helped to dehydrate the pasta rapidly.

Durum wheat is milled to produce semolina, a harder grain than common wheat, and it takes a good manufacturer of dry pasta to ensure that the production process actually translates into firm pasta when cooked. Ideally, dry pasta has a yellowish-golden hue derived from the natural colour of the durum wheat and a neutral flavour to absorb the sauces. Better brands have a meaty texture when cooked al dente—the point when the pasta is cooked yet still firm to the bite.

There are hundreds of dry pasta varieties in the world today, and they are all largely named for the shapes they represent. They are usually classified according to their physical appearances. Though there are no strict rules, these distinctions determine the sauces that go best with it. A long, thin pasta, for instance, is typically paired with a smooth sauce that will not overpower its delicate shape; while thick chunky shapes go well with a robust sauce with meaty flavours.

ABOVE: **Eggs and flour are staples of the classic Italian kitchen.**

BELOW: **Italians treasure tradition. From the mixing to the rolling of the dough, each step must be carefully carried out to achieve optimal results.**

Quality Pasta Makers

Though there are hundreds of pasta manufacturers in Italy today, only a few have established themselves internationally. Agnesi is one of them. Founded by the Agnesi family in 1824, the company quickly earned countrywide recognition for the remarkable output of its dry pasta factory, located in a small town on the shores of the Mediterranean sea which is known as Imperia today.

The company took full advantage of facilities at the nearby port and docks, and Agnesi became the most immediately recognisable dry pasta producer in the whole of the Liguria coastal stretch; in fact, it is little exaggeration to observe that the region somewhat owes part of its wealth to the businesses, jobs and opportunities that have sprung up around the Agnesi factories. Its entire business operations was praised as exemplary not only for the distinctive quality of its products, but also the sheer logistics orchestration that went into it.

Probably the oldest pasta producer in Italy, Agnesi is still firmly focussed on producing the quality dry pasta preferred by leading Italian chefs. It showcases tradition and expertise in its products which have found their way across the oceans to the United States, South America, and even around Asia, where appreciation for fine Italian cuisine is growing rapidly. It imports top quality durum wheat from around the world in order to guarantee a product that meets the expectations of the most demanding consumers. These include excellent cooking performance, perfect colour and great taste. And its in-house milling facilities produce fresh semolina that incorporates the protein-rich and highly nutritious wheat germ into Agnesi's quality pasta.

TOP: **Advertisements from the forties and fifties.**

ABOVE: **Agnesi combines tradition with technology to earn its stronghold in the ever-competitive pasta enterprise.**

RIGHT: **The emblem of Agnesi.**

Chef with a Cause

As rich as its history has been, the future of pasta is in good hands, given the likes of Diego Chiarini today. You'll even notice a fierce sparkle in his eye when the acclaimed chef discusses the finer aspects of Italian cuisine.

ABOVE: The restaurant's elegant and understated interior allows the chef's creations to speak volumes for themselves.

TOP LEFT: Diego Chiarini.

BELOW: Senso's courtyard melds nature and antiquity to invoke an authentic Italian ambience.

Chiarini's culinary calling was seeded as a boy growing on his family farm in North Italy; to which he still returns occasionally to help make wine with his father. He spent his holidays, however, under the watchful eyes of an uncle, who served as maître d' at a coastal restaurant. This experience left a deep and formative impression in the young Chiarini's head: of fresh countryside ingredients, simple but deliberate cooking, exhilarating seaside surroundings, and the allure of the traditional Italian way of life.

Thus fuelled by this romantic sensibility, the young man left home to pursue his culinary muse, on a quest that has seen him notably commended for service at top Italian kitchens around the world: the Royal Monceau Hotel in Paris, the Four Seasons Hotel in Milan, Hotel de Paris in Monaco and Bice at the Tokyo Four Seasons Hotel.

Of late, though, he has taken on restaurateur responsibilities as chef and partner of Senso restaurant in Singapore. So far, this venture has grown into a global Senso franchise, with sister restaurants in New Delhi and Geneva. His career is also marked with rave reviews and 'Best of' awards, throughout France, Japan and Singapore.

Chiarini explains that one's first encounter with a foreign culture is always through food, and his restaurant serves as his homeland's embassy. 'The food, even statues, music, décor and service, must be the maximum that you can offer,' he insists. To infuse his cooking with an authentic historicity—whether it's pasta, fish, tomato salad or wine, Chiarini is constantly researching the history, geography and culture of Italian cuisine, and maintains an antique cookbook collection from which he culls inspiration for his own kitchen. 'Follow your dream and believe it with humility and energy,' he says. 'This is my recipe.'

1. Farfalle
2. Sedanini
3. Penne
4. Orecchiette
5. Ditali rigati
6. Tortiglioni
7. Paccheri
8. Tagliolini
9. Spaghetti, linguine,
   fidelini and bucatini
10. Lasagne

Popular Types of Dry Pasta

Farfalle Pasta that is pinched in the middle to resemble a butterfly. Often recommended for salads and oil-based sauces.

Sedanini This is a North Italian pasta that resembles thin, slender celery stalks; after which it is named.

Penne Small tubes cut at an angle, taking its name from its tip which looks somewhat like a fountain pen nib.

Orecchiette Pasta shaped like small ears, best paired with thick vegetable or fish sauces.

Ditali rigati Translates as 'little thimbles', with ridges along its length, and is highly versatile as a base for soups, salads or stir-fried dishes.

Tortiglioni This tubular pasta with a spiralling surface and subtle twist is often served in casseroles or with robust and chunky sauces.

Paccheri Large pasta tubes, which trap sauces inside during cooking. The name translates as 'slaps', which is apparently the sound it makes after cooking, as you lift it with a fork.

Tagliolini The thinnest of ribbon noodles, also called 'tagliarini'.

Spaghetti The famous little string, or lengths of cord, pasta, which is very versatile in matching with sauces. Interestingly, the ubiquitous Spaghetti Bolognese is hardly encountered in Italy, being an unauthentic innovation abroad that has seduced the foreign palate.

Linguine Long and flat pasta strips about five millimetres wide; its name is derived from the Italian word for 'tongue'.

Fidelini Very fine noodles; fidelini actually means 'little worms'.

Bucatini This is a long pasta, similar to spaghetti except with a hollow centre, and its name means 'with a hole'.

Lasagne Flat pasta, used for building layers with sauce and ingredients in between. In Latin, 'lasanum' means 'pot'.

Fusilli A favourite for casseroles, this twisted shape catches sauce and bits of meat and vegetables in its threads. It can also be broken into smaller pieces for salads.

Maccheroni rigati Traditional tubular pasta, with lines along its side.

Tagliatelle mezzane Thin and flat ribbon noodles, relatively delicate. From the word 'tagliare', which means 'to cut'.

Pappardelle Pasta strips just over two centimetres wide, which sometimes come with a fluted edge. Originated from the word 'pappare', which means 'to gobble up'.

Conchiglioni Shell-shaped pasta, often cooked with green peas, crunchy bacon bits or other morsels that get nicely trapped inside.

Paglia e fieno 'Straw and hay'. A mixture of green and natural fettuccine (slightly thicker ribbon noodles) popular in the Emilia-Romagna region of Italy.

Fusilli

Maccheroni rigati

Tagliatelle mezzane

Pappardelle

Conchiglioni

Paglia e fieno

COOKING DRY PASTA: DO'S AND DON'TS

The skill of cooking pasta until it is optimally tender yet firm (in other words, al dente) is elusive to all but the most dedicated and experienced of chefs. However, you can begin your apprenticeship by following these simple steps.

Hot Pot

The cooking procedure is central to preparing al dente pasta, and a good chef will stand beside the stove to nurse and supervise the cooking of each portion from start to finish.

Always start with plenty of boiling water: picture a pot of water bubbling away in a lively simmer, ready to transform a handful of uncooked dry pasta into al dente delight. This also allows the pasta room to move freely, thus preventing the pieces from clumping together. As soon as the water starts boiling, salt it generously with one teaspoon of salt per litre of water; otherwise your pasta will end up tasting flat and lifeless. Never add oil, though, unless perhaps you are cooking stuffed fresh pasta which would otherwise stick together during cooking.

At this point, add the pasta and turn the heat up immediately, so the water reaches its boiling point again. Stir frequently to separate the pieces and make sure they all cook evenly.

Bite Test

Generally, it takes about eight minutes to cook noodles like spaghetti, and up to 12 minutes for short cuts like penne. But every shape has its own cooking time and the best way to check if the pasta is cooked is by biting on a piece about a minute or so before it is expected to be done. It should feel firm, and with no white chalky centre visible.

Repeat this until the pasta is judged to be al dente, and then remove it from the heat and strain, leaving just a bit of the cooking water still clinging to the pasta. Pasta will continue to cook even

TOP: **Adding ample salt to the water will ensure that your pasta is flavourful.**

ABOVE: **When the water starts bubbling, grab a handful of pasta and ease it into the pot.**

after it has been removed from the heat and strained, so you'll need to accomplish this quickly.

Never rinse pasta that is to be served hot: you will remove the outer layer of starch that lets the sauce stick to the noodle. Pasta prepared for salads, however, might be rinsed to stop it from cooking further in its own heat.

Dressing Up

Pasta should be dressed immediately after cooking: the hotter the pasta, the better it will absorb the sauce. It is never cooked ahead in any self-respecting restaurant. Ideally, you should warm the serving plates in preparation, then toss the pasta on these straight away or it will turn into a disappointing clump if left to stand naked for a few minutes. You might also want to set aside some of the cooking water, adding a few teaspoons to the pasta while dressing it, to keep it moist.

Fork, Wine and Opera

According to legend, the fork was invented by an official in the Bourbon Court of Naples as late as the 19th century, before which the local tradition called for Italians to eat pasta with their fingers. Spoons are not necessary unless you're tackling a runny sauce or find yourself at a formal dining event. Good wine and a lively opera recording, however, are considered mandatory in some circles.

ABOVE, EXTREME LEFT: Once the pasta becomes noticeably softer, wind a small amount onto a fork for the taste test. While it should taste cooked, it is important that the pasta remains al dente, or 'firm to the bite'.

ABOVE, LEFT: Start cooking the pasta only when the sauce is nearly ready so that both may be served hot.

ABOVE: When the pasta is cooked, strain, then add it to the sauce and toss.

OVEN-BAKED LASAGNE WITH THREE CHEESES AND PEAR

Lasagne Al Mascarpone-Gorgonzola-Parmigiano e Pere Cotte in Forno

INGREDIENTS

200 g mascarpone cheese
100 ml milk
salt and pepper
100 g butter, melted
400 g Agnesi lasagne
200 g Gorgonzola cheese, chopped
100 g Parmesan cheese, grated
50 g parsley, chopped
300 g pears, thinly sliced
freshly ground black pepper

PREPARATION [Serves 4 • Takes 50 minutes]

1. Preheat the oven at 200°C.
2. Combine the mascarpone cheese and milk in a bowl and mix well. Season to taste with salt and pepper, taking care not to add too much salt as the cheeses are already salty.
3. Grease a 20-by-20-by-4-cm baking dish with some melted butter, then line the base of the dish with a few pieces of Agnesi lasagne. Brush the lasagne with some melted butter and spread some of the mascarpone cheese and milk mixture on the lasagne. Sprinkle some Gorgonzola and Parmesan cheese, and parsley over, then top with some pear slices. (Set 4 slices aside for garnishing.) Cover with Agnesi lasagne and repeat the layering process with the remaining ingredients.
4. Brush the top layer of lasagne with butter and sprinkle some Parmesan cheese over. Top the lasagne with the 4 slices of pear and cover the dish with aluminum foil. Bake the lasagne for 30 minutes until the top turns golden brown.
5. Remove from the heat and cut the lasagne into 4 squares. Garnish each square with a slice of baked pear and a sprinkling of freshly ground black pepper to serve.

Substitute lasagne with conchiglioni. Just chop the pear instead of slicing it, then mix all the ingredients into a filling for the conchiglioni.

FARFALLE WITH ARTICHOKES AND MARJORAM BRAISED IN WHITE WINE

Farfalle Con Carciofi e Maggiorana al Vino Bianco Secco

INGREDIENTS

60 g garlic, peeled and chopped
40 g marjoram or oregano leaves
200 g whole artichokes, trimmed
100 ml Agnesi extra virgin olive oil
100 ml dry white wine
100 ml warm vegetable stock
320 g Agnesi farfalle
3 litres salted boiling water
80 g cherry tomatoes, quartered
salt and pepper

This dish may also be prepared with tortiglioni.

PREPARATION [Serves 4 • Takes 30 minutes]

1. In a saucepan, roast the garlic, a quarter of the marjoram or oregano leaves, and the artichokes (with stems on) in half the Agnesi extra virgin olive oil over low heat for 5 minutes.

2. Add the wine, then cover the pan with aluminum foil and cook for 5 more minutes.

3. Add the vegetable stock, then cover the pan again for 5 minutes until the artichokes are cooked. Remove the artichokes from the pan and set aside.

4. Cook the Agnesi farfalle in the salted boiling water for 6 minutes, then strain and add it to the sauce. Add the remaining olive oil and cherry tomatoes and toss well. Season to taste with salt and pepper.

5. Divide the pasta among 4 plates and garnish with the artichokes and remaining marjoram or oregano leaves to serve.

BUCATINI WITH TOMATO SAUCE, CAPERS AND LEMON ZEST

Bucatini in Salsa di Capperi, Limone a Buccia e Pomodoro in Salsa

INGREDIENTS

200 ml Agnesi tomato pulp or passeta (purée)
100 ml Agnesi extra virgin olive oil
60 g capers, chopped
280 g Agnesi bucatini
3 litres salted boiling water
60 g Parmesan cheese, grated
40 g parsley, chopped
40 g lemon zest (yellow part), thinly sliced
salt and pepper
40 g small capers with stems

PREPARATION [Serves 4 • Takes 30 minutes]

1. In a saucepan, warm the Agnesi tomato sauce and extra virgin olive oil, and chopped capers over low heat and mix well. Keep warm and covered until required.

2. Cook the Agnesi bucatini in the salted boiling water for 10 minutes, then strain and add it to the tomato mixture. Add the Parmesan cheese, parsley and half the lemon zest. Toss well for a few minutes. Season to taste with salt and pepper.

3. Poach the remaining lemon zest in the water used for cooking pasta for 2 minutes.

4. Arrange the pasta in a rectangular terrine (or roll it up with aluminum foil to form a cylinder). Place this in a warm place (e.g. on top of a heated oven) for a few minutes.

5. Remove the pasta from the terrine (or the aluminum foil) to a plate and garnish with the small capers with stems and poached lemon zest to serve.

Sigarette ziti may be used in place of bucatini.

SPAGHETTI CHITARRA WITH GREEN AND WHITE ASPARAGUS SAUCE

Spaghetti Chitarra e Asparagi Verdi con Crema di Asparagi Bianchi e Parmigiano

INGREDIENTS

160 g green asparagus, peeled
160 g white asparagus, peeled
3 litres salted boiling water
1 litre iced water
100 ml Agnesi extra virgin olive oil
80 g Parmesan cheese, grated
50 g leek, diced
320 g Agnesi spaghetti chitarra
salt and pepper
4 sprigs dill

PREPARATION [Serves 4 • Takes 25 minutes]

1. Cook the green and white asparagus in the salted boiling water for 7 minutes. Refresh them with iced water immediately.

2. Dice half the green asparagus and set the other half aside. Process the white asparagus with half the Agnesi extra virgin olive oil and Parmesan cheese in a blender to obtain a smooth purée. Set aside.

3. In a saucepan, sauté the leek and diced green asparagus in the remaining olive oil for a few minutes. Add some of the water used to cook the asparagus to keep the mixture moist.

4. Cook the Agnesi spaghetti chitarra in the same salted boiling water used to cook the asparagus for 4 minutes, then strain and add it to the sautéed leek and green asparagus. Add the white asparagus purée and toss well. Season to taste with salt and pepper.

5. Arrange the cooked whole asparagus on a plate as shown. Wrap some spaghetti chitarra around a big fork and slide the pasta onto the asparagus. Prepare 3 more portions. Garnish with the dill sprigs to serve.

Use festonate if spaghetti chitarra is not available.

SPAGHETTONI WITH MIXED VEGETABLES, ARUGULA AND BREADCRUMBS

Spaghettoni alle Verdure, Rucola in Foglie e Pane Tostato per Condire

INGREDIENTS

80 g eggplant, thinly sliced
80 g carrots, peeled and thinly sliced
40 g yellow capsicum, thinly sliced
40 g red capsicum, thinly sliced
80 g zucchini, thinly sliced
40 g leek, thinly sliced
80 g asparagus, thinly sliced
100 ml Agnesi extra virgin olive oil
2 tomatoes, chopped
300 ml warm vegetable stock
320 g Agnesi spaghettoni
3 litres salted boiling water
120 g arugula leaves
120 g breadcrumbs, toasted
salt and pepper

PREPARATION [Serves 4 • Takes 30 minutes]

1. In a saucepan, sauté all the vegetables in the Agnesi extra virgin olive oil over low heat for 10 minutes.
2. Add the tomatoes and vegetable stock, and put on the lid. Keep cooking for 10 minutes.
3. Cook the Agnesi spaghettoni in the salted boiling water for 8 minutes, then strain, and add it to the sauce. Add some arugula leaves and the breadcrumbs, and toss well over medium heat for 1 minute. Season to taste with salt and pepper.
4. Garnish with the remaining arugula leaves to serve.

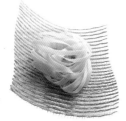

Tagliatelle mezzane may also be used to prepare this dish.

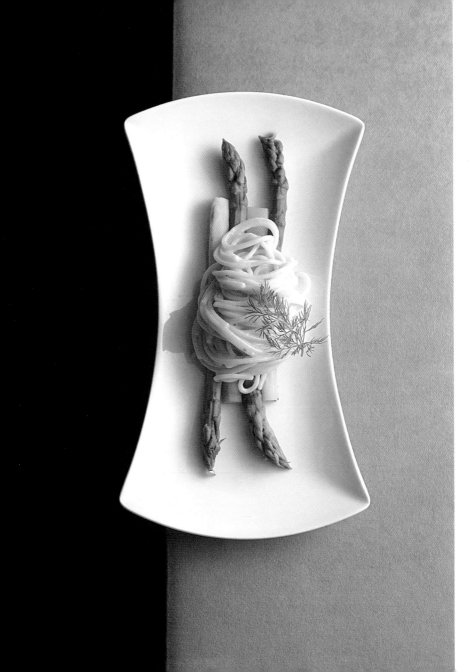

PENNE RIGATE WITH TOMATO AND CHILLI MARMALADE, AND LEMON ZEST

Penne Rigate alla Marmellata di Peperoncino e Buccia di Limone al Pomodoro

INGREDIENTS

1 lemon
100 ml Agnesi extra virgin olive oil
30 g garlic, peeled and chopped
80 g red chilli, seeded and chopped
300 g assorted tomatoes, peeled and chopped
80 ml honey
200 ml warm vegetable stock
320 g Agnesi penne rigate
3 litres salted boiling water
salt and pepper
4 stalks chives

PREPARATION [Serves 4 • Takes 50 minutes]

1. Peel the lemon and slice the yellow part of the zest into long, thin strips, then chop the lemon flesh.
2. Warm the Agnesi extra virgin olive oil in a saucepan over low heat and add the garlic, red chilli, tomatoes, lemon flesh, honey and vegetable stock. Mix well and put on the lid. Cook the mixture for 15 minutes.
3. Cook the Agnesi penne rigate in the salted boiling water for 8 minutes, then strain and add it to the sauce. Toss well for 2 minutes and season to taste with salt and pepper.
4. Poach the sliced lemon zest in the water used for cooking pasta for 2 minutes.
5. Divide the pasta among 4 plates and garnish with the poached lemon zest and chives to serve.

Penne rigate may be replaced with sedanini in this recipe.

FIDELINI TIMBALE WITH
MIXED CHEESE FONDUE AND BALSAMIC VINEGAR

Fidelini in Timballo con Fonduta di Formaggi Misti e Balsamico Ridotto

INGREDIENTS
100 ml hot milk
50 g Gorgonzola cheese, chopped
50 g Taleggio or mozzarella cheese, chopped
50 g fontina cheese, chopped
100 ml balsamic vinegar
30 ml honey
320 g Agnesi fidelini
3 litres salted boiling water
40 g parsley, chopped
salt and pepper
50 g butter, melted
80 g Parmesan cheese, grated

PREPARATION [Serves 4 • Takes 40 minutes]

1. Preheat the oven at 200°C.
2. In a saucepan, mix the milk with the cheeses, excluding the Parmesan, and melt over low heat for 15 minutes. Transfer half the cheese fondue into a bowl and keep warm until required.
3. In a separate saucepan, mix the balsamic vinegar and honey and reduce over low heat until a third of the orginal amount is left.
4. Cook the Agnesi fidelini in the salted boiling water for 3 minutes, then strain and add it to the cheese fondue in the pan. Add the parsley and mix well. Season to taste with salt and pepper, then cook over low heat for 2 minutes.
5. Grease 4 small stainless steel ring moulds with melted butter and place them on a baking tray. Fill them with the fidelini and cheese mixture and bake for 10 minutes.
6. Sprinkle the Parmesan cheese on a flat plate and cook it for 1 minute in the microwave set on 'high', until it turns golden brown. Remove from the heat and set aside to cool. When cool, break them into 4 wafers.
7. Divide the remaining cheese fondue among 4 plates, unmould the fidelini and place each portion on a plate. Drizzle the balsamic vinegar and honey mixture around and garnish with the Parmesan wafers to serve.

**Fidelini may be
replaced with capellini.**

DITALI RIGATI AND MIXED VEGETABLE SOUP BAKED IN BREAD CRUST

Ditali Rigati in Minestrone di Verdure Miste cotte al forno in Pane

INGREDIENTS

50 g onions, peeled and chopped
30 g garlic, peeled and chopped
50 g leek, cut into 1-cm cubes
100 ml Agnesi extra virgin olive oil
80 g carrots, peeled and cut into 1-cm cubes
100 g potatoes, cut into 1-cm cubes
50 g celery, cut into 1-cm cubes
80 g pumpkin, cut into 1-cm cubes
2 litres warm vegetable stock
120 g Agnesi ditali rigati
80 g tomatoes, seeded and cut into 1-cm cubes
80 g zucchini, cut into 1-cm cubes
30 g parsley, chopped
50 g broccoli, cut into small florets
4 round bread, crusty and very dry

PREPARATION [Serves 4 • Takes 70 minutes]

1. Preheat the oven at 200°C.
2. In a pot or deep saucepan, sauté the onions, garlic and leek in some of the Agnesi extra virgin olive oil for 5 minutes, then add the carrots and potatoes and sauté for 5 minutes.
3. Add the celery and pumpkin, and enough vegetable stock to cover all the ingredients. Cook over low heat for 30 minutes.
4. Add the Agnesi ditali rigati, tomatoes, zucchini, parsley and broccoli, and cook for 6 minutes.
5. Cut off the tops of the bread and remove the white insides. Pour the soup into the hollowed bread and mix in some of the remaining olive oil. Bake for 5 minutes before serving.

For a more substantial meal, substitute ditali rigati with paccheri.

FUSILLI WITH PAN-FRIED PORCINI MUSHROOMS, APPLES AND FRESH THYME

Fusilli ai Funghi Porcini, Mele e Timo in Foglie

INGREDIENTS

20 g garlic, peeled and sliced
80 g onions, peeled and chopped
50 g thyme leaves
100 ml Agnesi extra virgin olive oil
200 g porcini mushrooms, sliced
100 g green apples, diced
500 ml dry white wine
salt and pepper
320 g Agnesi fusilli
3 litres salted boiling water
60 g Parmesan cheese, grated
4 sprigs thyme

PREPARATION [Serves 4 • Takes 20 minutes]

1. In a saucepan, sauté the garlic, onions and thyme leaves in half the Agnesi extra virgin olive oil over low heat for a few minutes until the onions are translucent.
2. Add the porcini and cook for 8 minutes, then add the green apples and white wine. Season to taste with salt and pepper, and simmer the mixture until the wine evaporates.
3. Cook the Agnesi fusilli in the salted boiling water for 8 minutes, then strain and add it to the porcini mixture. Add the remaining olive oil and Parmesan cheese, and toss well.
4. Divide the pasta among 4 plates and garnish with the thyme sprigs to serve.

Substitute fusilli with pappardelle.

FUSILLI RIGATI WITH BASIL AND
BEETROOT PESTO AND PAN-FRIED PRAWNS

Fusilli Rigati al Pesto Rosso di Basilico-Barbabietola e Gamberetti

PREPARATION [Serves 4 • Takes 30 minutes]

1. Process the beetroot, basil leaves, garlic, pinenuts and a third of the Agnesi extra virgin olive oil in a blender to obtain a smooth creamy sauce. Season to taste with salt and pepper.
2. Season the prawns with salt and pepper. In a saucepan, sauté them in the remaining olive oil until they are cooked. Add the white wine and simmer until almost all of the wine has evaporated. Put the lid on and keep warm until required.
3. Cook the Agnesi fusilli rigati in the salted boiling water for 6 minutes, then strain and add it to the prawns. Toss well and cook the mixture over medium heat for 1 minute.
4. Add the basil and beetroot pesto to the pasta and toss well.
5. Divide the pasta and prawns among 4 plates and garnish with the basil sprigs to serve.

INGREDIENTS

60 g beetroot, boiled
60 g basil leaves
20 g garlic, peeled and chopped
20 g pinenuts, toasted
100 ml Agnesi extra virgin olive oil
salt and pepper
160 g prawns, shells removed
100 ml dry white wine
320 g Agnesi fusilli rigati
3 litres salted boiling water
4 sprigs basil

**As an alternative, prepare
this recipe with farfalle.**

SPAGHETTI WITH MIXED SEAFOOD AND CHERRY TOMATOES

Spaghetti ai Frutti di Mare e Pomodorini Ciliegia

PREPARATION [Serves 4 • Takes 20 minutes]

1. Sauté the garlic and salted anchovies in the Agnesi extra virgin olive oil over low heat until the garlic turns lightly brown, then add the clams and mussels. Toss well, put on the lid and cook the mixture for 4 minutes until the shellfish open.
2. Cook the Agnesi spaghetti in the salted boiling water for 6 minutes, then strain and set aside.
3. Add the crabmeat, prawns, scallops and squid to the shellfish and sauté for 4 minutes.
4. Add the white wine and simmer until the wine evaporates, then add the cooked pasta followed by the cherry tomatoes. Toss well and season to taste with salt and pepper.
5. Add the chopped parsley and toss well.
6. Divide the pasta among 4 plates and arrange the cherry tomatoes and seafood around. Serve the scallops in the shells and garnish each plate with 2 chive stalks.

INGREDIENTS

30 g garlic, peeled and sliced thinly
20 g salted anchovies, chopped
100 ml Agnesi extra virgin olive oil
40 g clams, with shells
40 g mussels, with shells
320 g Agnesi spaghetti
3 litres salted boiling water
40 g crabmeat
60 g baby prawns
120 g scallops, without shells
40 g baby squid
100 ml dry white wine
120 g cherry tomatoes, quartered
salt and pepper
40 g parsley, chopped
4 scallop shells
8 stalks chives

Substitute spaghetti
with tagliolini.

TAGLIATELLE MEZZANE WITH CAPSICUM SAUCE AND LOBSTER

Tagliatelle Mezzane in Salsa Peperone Dolce e Aragosta

INGREDIENTS

200 g red capsicums, seeded
200 g ripe tomatoes
100 g onions, peeled and chopped
20 g garlic, peeled and chopped
200 ml Agnesi extra virgin olive oil
salt and pepper
4 (200 to 300 g each) lobsters, with shells
30 g dried oregano
100 ml dry white wine
320 g Agnesi tagliatelle mezzane
3 litres salted boiling water

PREPARATION [Serves 4 • Takes 50 minutes]

1. Combine the capsicums, tomatoes, onions, garlic and 75 ml of the Agnesi extra virgin olive oil in a casserole. Mix well and season to taste with salt and pepper. Cover the casserole and cook over low heat for 30 minutes.

2. Separate the lobster shells from the meat, chop half the shells and set them aside. In a saucepan, sauté the remaining half shells in 50 ml of the olive oil until they are cooked, then set aside for garnishing. Cut the lobster meat into medallions.

3. Combine the chopped and sautéed shells and the remaining olive oil in the same pan and warm over low heat for 20 minutes to flavour the olive oil.

4. When the ingredients in the casserole are ready, remove the capsicums and process them in a blender to obtain a smooth purée. Pass the purée through a fine-mesh sieve. Set aside.

5. When the lobster oil is ready, remove from the heat and strain.

6. In the same pan, sauté the lobster medallions and dried oregano in the lobster oil. Add the white wine and simmer until the wine has evaporated.

7. Cook the Agnesi tagliatelle mezzane in the salted boiling water for 4 minutes, then strain and add to the pan. Add the capsicum purée and toss well. Season to taste with salt and pepper.

8. Arrange each portion of pasta in half a cooked lobster shell to serve.

This dish may also be prepared with linguine.

PENNE, BUTTER LETTUCE AND TOMATO SALAD WITH CAVIAR DRESSING

Penne in Insalata con Lattuga, Pomodoro a Cubetti e Caviale

INGREDIENTS

320 g Agnesi penne
3 litres salted boiling water
200 ml Agnesi extra virgin olive oil
4 heads butter lettuce
juice from 1 lemon
40 g chives, chopped
40 g Sevruga caviar
salt and pepper
200 g ripe tomatoes, cut into cubes
40 g red radish, sliced

PREPARATION [Serves 4 • Takes 30 minutes]

1. Cook the Agnesi penne in the salted boiling water for 6 minutes, then strain and toss it in half the Agnesi extra virgin olive oil to prevent it from sticking together.
2. Clean the butter lettuce and remove the centre of each head without breaking off the outer layers. Keep refrigerated until required.
3. Prepare the salad dressing by mixing the lemon juice, remaining olive oil, chives and Sevruga caviar. Season to taste with salt and pepper.
4. Mix the pasta with the tomatoes, red radish and one-third of the dressing. Fill each lettuce head with the mixture.
5. Place each lettuce head on a plate and drizzle the remaining dressing around to serve.

Eliche tricolore may be used in place of penne.

ORECCHIETTE WITH PRAWNS, SAFFRON, ZUCCHINI AND ORANGE ZEST

Orecchiette ai Gamberi, Zafferano in Pistilli, Zucchine e Buccia di Arancia

PREPARATION [Serves 4 • Takes 25 minutes]

1. Peel the orange and slice the orange part of the zest thinly. Squeeze the juice from the orange and discard the pulp. Set the juice aside.
2. In a saucepan, sauté the zucchini in the Agnesi extra virgin olive oil over low heat for 5 minutes, then add the prawns. Sauté for a few minutes, then add the saffron and the orange juice. Mix well and reduce the orange juice by half.
3. Cook the Agnesi orecchiette in the salted boiling water for 10 minutes, then strain and add it to the zucchini mixture. Add the chopped parsley and toss for a few more minutes. Season to taste with salt and pepper.
4. Divide the pasta among 4 plates and garnish with the sliced orange zest to serve.

INGREDIENTS

1 orange
200 g green zucchini, diced
100 ml Agnesi extra virgin olive oil
200 g prawns
3 g saffron threads
320 g Agnesi orecchiette
3 litres salted boiling water
30 g parsley, chopped
salt and pepper

Use paglia e fieno if orecchiette is unavailable.

SIGARETTE ZITI WITH BROCCOLI PESTO AND SEA SCALLOPS

Sigarette Ziti al Pesto di Broccoli e Cappesante

PREPARATION [Serves 4 • Takes 30 minutes]

1. Poach the broccoli in the salted boiling water for 8 minutes, then refresh it in the iced water immediately. Strain, pat dry with kitchen tissue and chop.
2. In a saucepan, sauté the garlic, red chilli and scallops in the Agnesi extra virgin olive oil over medium heat until the garlic turns crispy and golden brown.
3. Add the white wine and simmer until the wine has evaporated. Remove the scallops from the pan and keep warm until required. Add the broccoli, parsley and tomatoes to the pan and toss well.
4. Cook the Agnesi sigarette ziti in the same salted boiling water used to cook the broccoli for 8 minutes, then strain and add it to the broccoli mixture. Toss for a few minutes, then season to taste with salt and pepper.
5. Divide the pasta among 4 plates and garnish with the scallops to serve.

INGREDIENTS

240 g broccoli
3 litres salted boiling water
1 litre iced water
60 g garlic, peeled and chopped
40 g red chilli, seeds removed and chopped
160 g scallops, without shells
100 ml Agnesi extra virgin olive oil
100 ml dry white wine
40 g parsley, chopped
60 g tomatoes, seeds removed and diced
320 g Agnesi sigarette ziti
salt and pepper

You may also use orecchiette to prepare this dish.

PAN-FRIED SPAGHETTINI AND
SILVER FISH TIMBALE WITH TOMATO JUICE

Spaghettini e Gianchetti al Salto con Passata di Pomodoro e Origano

INGREDIENTS

120 g ripe tomatoes
60 g celery, chopped
200 ml Agnesi extra virgin olive oil
40 g oregano leaves
salt and pepper
320 g Agnesi spaghettini
3 litres salted boiling water
160 g small silver fish
1 egg white
4 sprigs rosemary or tarragon

PREPARATION [Serves 4 • Takes 20 minutes]

1. Process the tomatoes, celery, half the Agnesi extra virgin olive oil and half the oregano leaves in a blender to obtain a smooth purée. Season to taste with salt and pepper, then pass the mixture through a fine-mesh sieve. Keep warm until required.

2. Cook the Agnesi spaghettini in the salted boiling water for 3 minutes, then strain and mix it with the small silver fish, egg white and remaining oregano leaves. Season to taste with salt and pepper.

3. In a non-stick saucepan, fry the pasta mixture in the remaining olive oil over medium heat for 1½ minutes, spreading the pasta around the pan evenly. When the bottom of the pasta turns crispy and golden brown, turn it over carefully. Fry the other side for 1½ minutes until it turns crispy and golden brown as well.

4. Remove the pasta from the pan to a flat surface carefully and use a stainless steel ring mould to cut 4 pasta circles as shown.

5. Spoon the warm tomato purée on 4 plates and place each pasta circle on a plate. Garnish with rosemary or tarragon sprigs to serve.

Fidelini may also be used for this dish.

FESTONATE WITH EGGPLANT AND GARLIC SAUCE, AND SEARED TUNA

Festonate al Ragú di Tonno, Melazane e Aglio Dolce

INGREDIENTS

800 g eggplants
80 g garlic, peeled
juice from 1 lemon
100 ml Agnesi extra virgin olive oil
salt and pepper
320 g Agnesi festonate
3 litres salted boiling water
200 g fresh tuna, cut into big cubes

Festonate may be replaced with pappardelle.

PREPARATION [Serves 4 • Takes 35 minutes]

1. Preheat the oven at 200°C.
2. Bake the eggplants whole for 20 minutes.
3. Fill a small pot with water and bring to the boil. Add the garlic and bring the water to the boil again. Strain and set the garlic aside. Fill the pot with fresh water and bring to the boil. Add the garlic and bring to the boil again. Repeat this step 3 more times using fresh water to poach the garlic each time.
4. When the eggplants are ready, remove from the heat and separate the flesh from the skin. Slice the skin into long thin strips.
5. Process the eggplant flesh, poached garlic, lemon juice and two-thirds of the Agnesi extra virgin olive oil in a blender to obtain a smooth purée. Season to taste with salt and pepper.
6. Cook the Agnesi festonate in the salted boiling water for 6 minutes, then strain and set it aside.
7. In a non-stick saucepan, sear the tuna cubes in the remaining olive oil on all sides but keep the insides raw. Season to taste with salt and pepper, add the eggplant purée and cooked pasta. Toss for a few more minutes.
8. Divide the pasta among 4 plates and garnish with the eggplant skin to serve.

TAGLIOLINI WITH BLACK TRUFFLE, ANCHOVY AND SPRING ONION RAGOUT

Tagliolini in Salsa di Tartufo Nero, Cipollotti e Acciughe

INGREDIENTS

30 g garlic, peeled and chopped
30 g anchovies, chopped
60 ml Agnesi extra virgin olive oil
80 g spring onions, roots removed
60 g black truffles, chopped
80 ml water
320 g Agnesi tagliolini
3 litres salted boiling water
salt and pepper
30 g Parmesan shavings

PREPARATION [Serves 4 • Takes 25 minutes]

1. In a saucepan, cook the garlic and anchovies in the Agnesi extra virgin olive oil over low heat for 10 minutes, keeping the lid on.
2. Separate the green and white parts of the spring onions. Slice the green part and set aside.
3. Add the black truffles, remaining spring onions and water to the pan. Let the mixture cook uncovered for 10 minutes.
3. Cook the Agnesi tagliolini in the salted boiling water for 4 minutes, then strain and add it to the sauce. Toss well and season to taste with salt and pepper.
4. Divide the pasta among 4 serving dishes. Garnish with the sliced spring onions and Parmesan shavings to serve.

Use spaghetti chitarra if tagliolini is unavailable.

LINGUINE WITH SQUID INK SAUCE AND CLAMS

Linguine al Nero di Seppia e Vongole Veraci

INGREDIENTS

30 g garlic, peeled and chopped
20 g dried red chilli, chopped
60 g leeks, diced
100 ml Agnesi extra virgin olive oil
400 g clams, with shells
30 g parsley, chopped
100 ml dry white wine
10 ml squid ink
320 g Agnesi linguine
3 litres salted boiling water
salt and pepper
12 sprigs dill

PREPARATION [Serves 4 • Takes 25 minutes]

1. In a saucepan, sauté the garlic, dried red chilli and leeks in half the Agnesi extra virgin olive oil until the garlic is lightly browned, then add the clams, parsley and white wine. Cook for a few minutes until the clams open and the wine evaporates.

2. Remove the clams and keep warm until required. Add the squid ink to the sauce and mix well. Keep warm until required.

3. Cook the Agnesi linguine in the salted boiling water for 5 minutes, then strain and add it to the sauce. Add the remaining olive oil and toss for a few minutes. Season to taste with salt and pepper.

4. Divide the pasta among 4 plates and arrange the clams on the side. Garnish with the dill sprigs to serve.

**Linguine may be
replaced with fusilli rigati.**

MEZZE PENNE WITH BRAISED VEAL SHANK, LAMBRUSCO WINE AND PECORINO CHEESE

Mezze Penne al Brasato di Ossobuco, Lambrusco e Pecorino Stagionato

INGREDIENTS

1 kg veal shank
60 g plain flour
30 g onions, peeled and chopped
30 g carrots, peeled and chopped
30 g celery, chopped
60 g soft butter
salt and pepper
200 ml Lambrusco wine
320 g Agnesi mezze penne
3 litres salted boiling water
20 g garlic, peeled and chopped
20 g rosemary leaves, chopped
120 g pecorino cheese, sliced
20 g lemon zest (yellow part only), grated
4 sprigs rosemary

PREPARATION [Serves 4 • Takes 40 minutes]

1. Preheat the oven at 200°C.
2. Dust the veal shank on all sides with plain flour.
3. In a pot, sauté the onions, carrots and celery in the soft butter over medium heat for 5 minutes, then add the veal shank and roast for 10 minutes. Season to taste with salt and pepper.
4. Add the Lambrusco wine, put on the lid, then transfer the pot to the oven and cook the mixture for 60 minutes.
5. Remove the pot from the oven and peel the meat from the bone. Discard the bone and shred the meat, then add it to the vegetables in the pot. Mix well.
5. Cook the Agnesi mezze penne in the salted boiling water for 7 minutes, then strain and add it to the sauce.
6. Add the garlic and rosemary leaves and some pecorino cheese. (Set 4 slices of pecorino cheese aside for garnishing.) Season to taste with salt and pepper, then return the pot to the heat. Mix for 1 minute.
7. Divide the pasta among 4 plates and sprinkle some grated lemon zest over. Garnish each portion with a slice of pecorino cheese and a rosemary sprig to serve.

As an alternative, prepare this recipe with spaghettoni.

PAGLIA E FIENO WITH GREEN PEA RAGOUT AND PAN-FRIED HAM CUBES

Paglia e Fieno al Ragú di Piselli Spellati e Cubetti di Prosciutto Cotto

PREPARATION [Serves 4 • Takes 30 minutes]

1. Process the tomatoes in a blender to obtain a smooth purée.
2. Poach the green peas in the salted boiling water for 4 minutes, then remove from the water with a strainer.
3. In a saucepan, sauté the cooked ham and garlic in the Agnesi extra virgin olive oil over low heat for 5 minutes, then add the green peas, spinach leaves and white wine. Cook until the wine has evaporated.
4. Add the tomato purée and chives, and mix well. Season to taste with salt and pepper.
5. Cook the Agnesi paglia e fieno in the same salted boiling water used to cook the green peas for 4 minutes, then strain and add it to the sauce. Toss well for 2 minutes.
6. Divide the pasta among 4 plates, spoon the sauce over and arrange the ham cubes on the side to serve.

INGREDIENTS
80 g ripe tomatoes
240 g green peas
3 litres salted boiling water
120 g cooked ham, cut into big cubes
30 g garlic, peeled and chopped
100 ml Agnesi extra virgin olive oil
120 g spinach leaves, shredded
100 ml dry white wine
20 g chives, chopped
salt and pepper
320 g Agnesi paglia e fieno

**Substitute paglia e fieno
with penne rigate.**

CAMPAGNOLE WITH BRAISED CHICKEN AND BLACK OLIVES

Campagnole al Ragú di Pollo e Olive Nere Taggiasche

INGREDIENTS

1 spring chicken
salt and pepper
120 g shallots, peeled
30 g butter
10 g plain flour
30 g thyme leaves
80 g preserved black olives (without seeds)
500 ml Agnesi extra virgin olive oil
320 g Agnesi campagnole
3 litres salted boiling water
40 g tomatoes, peeled, seeds removed and diced
40 g Parmesan cheese, grated
4 sprigs thyme

PREPARATION [Serves 4 • Takes 50 minutes]

1. Season the spring chicken with salt and pepper. Place it in a pot and add enough water to cover the chicken completely. Add the shallots and bring to the boil. Cook the chicken in the boiling water for 35 minutes.
2. Remove the chicken and shallots from the pot and set the stock aside. Discard the shallots.
3. Debone the chicken, then shred the meat.
4. In a saucepan, melt the butter over low heat, then add the plain flour and mix well. Add 300 ml of chicken stock and simmer until the mixture is reduced to half its original amount.
5. In a separate pan, sauté the shredded chicken, thyme leaves and black olives in the Agnesi extra virgin olive oil for a few minutes.
6. Cook the Agnesi campagnole in the salted boiling water for 7 minutes, then strain and add it to the reduced chicken stock mixture and toss well.
7. Add the sautéed chicken mixture and toss for a few minutes.
8. Add the tomatoes and Parmesan cheese, and toss well. Season to taste with salt and pepper.
9. Divide the pasta among 4 plates and garnish with the thyme sprigs to serve.

This dish may also be prepared with penne.

OVEN-BAKED CONCHIGLIONI
WITH RICOTTA, PORK SAUSAGE AND VEGETABLE FILLING

Conchiglioni Farciti di Ricotta e Salsiccia al forno con Verdure Brasate

INGREDIENTS

80 g pork sausage meat
80 g ricotta cheese
40 g butter, diced
10 g cumin powder
80 g carrots, peeled and chopped
80 g onions, peeled and chopped
80 g celery, chopped
20 g rosemary leaves, chopped
30 g garlic, peeled and chopped
240 g Agnesi conchiglioni
3 litres salted boiling water
120 g tomatoes, peeled and chopped
100 ml dry white wine
salt and pepper
20 g sage leaves

PREPARATION [Serves 4 • Takes 40 minutes]

1. Preheat the oven at 200°C.
2. Mix the pork sausage meat with the ricotta cheese and keep refrigerated until required.
3. Combine the butter, cumin powder, carrots, onions, celery, rosemary leaves and garlic in a saucepan and put on the lid. Simmer over low heat for 20 minutes.
4. Cook the Agnesi conchiglioni in the salted boiling water for 4 minutes, then strain and set it aside for 5 minutes. Fill each conchiglioni with the sausage and ricotta mixture.
5. Add the tomatoes to the vegetable mixture in the pan, followed by the stuffed conchiglioni and white wine. Season to taste with salt and pepper, then put on the lid. Transfer the pan to the oven and cook the mixture for 6 minutes until almost all the wine has evaporated.
6. Divide the conchiglioni among 4 plates and spoon the sauce over. Garnish with the sage leaves to serve.

Substitute conchiglioni with lasagne. Just line a 20-by-20-by-4-cm baking dish with lasagne and layer the pasta alternately with the pork sausage and vegetable fillings.

TORTIGLIONI WITH LAMB SHANK RAGOUT AND OVEN-BAKED APPLE

Tortiglioni al Ragú di Agnello al forno con Mele Rosse

INGREDIENTS

1 lamb shank
200 ml Agnesi extra virgin olive oil
320 g leek, chopped
30 g rosemary leaves, chopped
salt and pepper
200 ml dry white wine
300 ml warm vegetable stock
4 apples, diced
320 g Agnesi tortiglioni
3 litres salted boiling water

PREPARATION [Serves 4 • Takes 60 minutes]

1. Preheat the oven at 200℃.
2. Pan-fry the lamb shank on all sides in half the Agnesi extra virgin olive oil for 10 minutes, then add the leek and rosemary leaves. Season to taste with salt and pepper, and cover the pan with aluminum foil. Transfer the pan to the oven and cook the mixture for 10 minutes.
3. Remove the pan from the oven, add the white wine, then cover and return to the oven for 5 minutes.
4. Remove the pan from the oven, add the vegetable stock, then cover and return to the oven for 10 minutes.
5. Remove the pan from the oven, add the apples, then cover and return to the oven for 10 minutes.
6. Remove the pan from the oven and set aside to cool slightly.
7. Debone the lamb shank and shred the meat. Mix the meat with the sauce and toss well.
8. Cook the Agnesi tortiglioni in the salted boiling water for 7 minutes, then strain and add it to the sauce. Toss for 2 minutes. Season to taste with salt and pepper.
9. Divide the pasta among 4 plates and serve hot.

Use fusilli if tortiglioni is unavailable.

ELICHE TRICOLORI WITH MEAT JUICE AND PAN-FRIED PANCETTA

Eliche Tricolori al Sugo d'Arrosto e Pancetta Soffritta

INGREDIENTS
400 g beef bones
20 g garlic, peeled
80 g soft butter
50 g plain flour
40 g carrots, peeled and diced
40 g onions, peeled and diced
40 g celery, diced
100 ml red wine
200 ml warm vegetable stock
320 g Agnesi eliche tricolori
3 litres salted boiling water
120 g pancetta (Italian bacon), sliced
30 g rosemary leaves, chopped
salt and pepper
4 celery leaves

PREPARATION [Serves 4 • Takes 40 minutes]

1. Preheat the oven at 200°C.
2. In a non-stick saucepan, roast the beef bones and garlic in the soft butter for a few minutes, then add the plain flour and cook for a few more minutes. Add the carrots, onions and celery, and mix for 5 minutes.
3. Add the red wine and simmer until the wine has evaporated. Add the vegetable stock and cover the pan with a sheet of aluminum foil.
4. Transfer the pan to the oven and cook the mixture for another 45 minutes.
5. Remove the pan from the heat, strain the roasting juices and set aside. Discard the bones.
6. Cook the Agnesi eliche tricolori in the salted boiling water for 7 minutes, then strain and set it aside.
7. Pan-fry the pancetta in a non-stick pan until crispy, then discard the fat from the pan. Remove the pancetta to a plate lined with kitchen tissue to absorb the excess oil.
8. Add the roasting juices, cooked pasta and rosemary leaves to the pan and toss well for a few minutes. Season to taste with salt and pepper.
9. Divide the pasta among 4 plates and garnish each portion with a slice of pancetta and a celery leaf to serve.

Spaghetti may also be used to prepare this dish.

SEDANINI AND BLACK ONION CONFIT WRAPPED IN PARMA HAM

Sedanini al Prosciutto Crudo e Cipolla Nera al Cumino

INGREDIENTS

800 g onions, peeled and sliced
80 g soft butter
50 g cumin powder
100 ml dry white wine
salt and pepper
320 g Parma ham, sliced thinly
320 g Agnesi sedanini
3 litres salted boiling water
40 g parsley, chopped
40 g Parmesan cheese, grated
4 sprigs rosemary

PREPARATION [Serves 4 • Takes 70 minutes]

1. Combine the onions, soft butter and 30 g of cumin powder in a saucepan and warm over low heat for 45 minutes. Keep stirring the mixture with a wooden spatula to mix well.
2. Add the white wine and season to taste with salt and pepper. Put on the lid and cook for 15 minutes.
3. Line 4 soup bowls with the Parma ham.
4. Cook the Agnesi sedanini in salted boiling water for 8 minutes, then strain and mix it with the onion mixture, parsley and Parmesan cheese. Season to taste with salt and pepper.
5. Fill the soup bowls with the pasta and wrap them up with the Parma ham. Overturn each portion onto a plate.
6. Garnish with the rosemary sprigs and the remaining cumin powder to serve.

Mezze penne may also be used to prepare this dish.

ORANGE-FLAVOURED PAPPARDELLE WITH BRAISED DUCK LEG

Pappardelle al Brasato di Anatra e Vin Cotto all'Arancio

INGREDIENTS

6 ripe oranges
4 (200 g each) duck legs
200 g carrots, peeled and diced
60 g garlic, peeled
10 g juniper berries
100 g plain flour
200 ml Agnesi extra virgin olive oil
300 ml mild red wine
280 g Agnesi pappardelle
3 litres salted boiling water
120 g Parmesan cheese, grated
salt and pepper
8 slices orange, seeds removed
50 g sugar
4 sprigs chervil

PREPARATION [Serves 4 • Takes 14 hours]

1. Preheat the oven at 200°C.
2. Peel the oranges, squeeze out the juice and set the juice aside. Chop the pulp and marinate the duck legs in the chopped pulp, carrots, garlic and juniper berries for 12 hours.
3. Remove the duck legs from the marinade and dust them with plain flour. Pan-fry them in half the Agnesi extra virgin olive oil for 10 minutes until they are crispy and golden brown.
4. Sauté the marinade ingredients in the remaining olive oil until they are cooked.
5. Add the duck to the marinade ingredients and sauté for another 5 minutes. Add the red wine and orange juice, then put on the lid. Place the pan in the oven and cook the mixture for 1 hour.
6. Remove from the heat and set aside to cool. Process all the ingredients, except the duck legs, in a blender to obtain a smooth purée. (Instead of serving the legs whole, you may also blend the duck meat with the other ingredients.)
7. Cook the Agnesi pappardelle in the salted boiling water for 6 minutes, then strain and add it to the sauce. Add the Parmesan cheese and toss well. Season to taste with salt and pepper.
8. While the pasta is cooking, place the orange slices in a pan and sprinkle the sugar on both sides. Pan-fry until the sugar caramelises, then remove from the pan and set aside to cool.
9. Divide the pasta among 4 plates and place a duck leg, a sprig of chervil and 2 slices of orange on the side to serve.

Maccheroni rigati may used in place of pappardelle.

MACCHERONI RIGATI WITH OXTAIL BRAISED IN BAROLO WIN

Maccheroni Rigati al Brasato di Coda di Bue al Barolo

PREPARATION [Serves 4 • Takes 2 hours]

1. Preheat the oven at 200°C.
2. Combine all the ingredients, except the pecorino cheese, Agnesi maccheroni rigati, salted boiling water, salt and pepper, in a saucepan and mix well. Place the pan in the oven and cook the mixture for 1½ hours.
3. Remove from the heat and set aside to cool. Debone the oxtail and shred the meat. Return the shredded meat to the pan and toss well, ensuring that the oil and red wine are still separated. Warm the mixture on the stove over low heat.
4. Cook the Agnesi maccheroni rigati in salted boiling water for 8 minutes, then strain and add it to the sauce. Add the pecorino cheese and mix for a few minutes. Season to taste with salt and pepper.
5. Divide the pasta among 4 plates and serve immediately.

INGREDIENTS

600 g oxtail, with bone
300 ml Barolo wine
150 ml Agnesi extra virgin olive oil
200 g tomatoes
60 g carrots, peeled and diced
60 g onions, peeled and diced
60 g celery, diced
40 g pecorino cheese, grated
320 g Agnesi maccheroni rigati
3 litres salted boiling water
salt and pepper

Substitute maccheroni rigati with bucatini.

GRATINATED SABAYON AND PACCHERI
WITH CARAMELISED STRAWBERRIES

Paccheri Farciti di Fragole Caramellate e Gratinati con uno Zabaione Classico

INGREDIENTS

140 g sugar
20 g butter
180 g strawberries, diced
240 g Agnesi paccheri
3 litres salted boiling water
2 egg yolks
300 ml milk

PREPARATION [Serves 4 • Takes 40 minutes]

1. Preheat the oven (turn on the top heating only) at 200°C.
2. In a non-stick saucepan, warm 40 g of sugar and the butter over medium heat until the mixture turns golden brown. Add the strawberries, mix well and cook for 8 minutes. Keep warm until required.
3. Cook the Agnesi paccheri in the salted boiling water for 6 minutes, then strain and arrange them, standing side by side, in an oven-proof dish.
4. Spoon the strawberry mixture over and fill each paccheri with some strawberries.
5. Whisk the eggs yolks with 60 g of sugar and the milk in a mixing bowl held over a basin of hot water for 10 minutes until the mixture is light and creamy.
6. Spoon the egg mixture on the pasta, sprinkle the remaining sugar over and bake for 15 minutes until the top turns golden brown. Remove from the oven and serve immediately.

Try preparing this dish with ditali rigati. Just toss the cooked pasta with the strawberry mixture before baking.

OVEN-BAKED CAPELLINI AND CREAM CAKE
WITH BLACK FIGS AND CINNAMON POWDER

Capellini al forno in Torta di Crema Pasticcera, Fichi Neri e Cannella in Polvere

INGREDIENTS

100 ml milk
1 egg yolk
55 g sugar
15 g plain flour
240 g Agnesi capellini
2 litres salted boiling water
20 g cinnamon powder
12 ripe black figs
30 g soft butter

PREPARATION [Serves 4 • Takes 40 minutes]

1. Preheat the oven at 200°C.
2. In a saucepan, bring the milk to the boil.
3. In a separate saucepan, combine the egg yolk with 25 g of sugar and the plain flour, and mix well with a wooden spatula. Slowly add the warm milk and mix well to obtain a smooth texture and creamy consistency.
4. Cook the Agnesi capellini in the salted boiling water for 1 minute, then strain and add it to the egg mixture. Add the cinnamon powder and toss well.
5. Fill a non-stick baking dish with the pasta. Make indentations that are deep enough to contain a fig on the pasta's surface.
6. Fill the indentations with the figs, sprinkle the remaining sugar over and brush the soft butter on the pasta. Bake in the oven for 15 minutes until the top turns golden brown.
7. Remove the pasta from the oven and use a stainless steel ring cutter to cut 4 pasta circles as shown. Serve each portion with the fig's baking juices on the side

This dish may also be prepared with spaghettini.

...IC SAUCES

...ES, BLACK ...AND CAPERS

...a

INGREDIENTS

30 g ...ic, peeled and sliced
50 g capers
5 g dried red chilli
30 g dried oregano
500 ml Agnesi extra virgin olive oil
500 ml dry white wine
500 g tomatoes, peeled and puréed
50 g black olives
10 g lemon zest, grated
salt and pepper

PREPARATION [Serves 4 • Takes 20 minutes]

1. Sauté the garlic, capers, dried red chilli and dried oregano in the Agnesi extra virgin olive oil for 5 minutes, then add the white wine and cook until the wine has evaporated.
2. Add the tomato purée, black olives and lemon zest. Season to taste with salt and pepper and mix well.
3. Cook the sauce over low heat for another 15 minutes.

PORCINI WITH THYME AND RED WINE

Di Porcini

INGREDIENTS

300 g porcini mushrooms, sliced
500 ml Agnesi extra virgin olive oil
20 g thyme leaves
30 g potatoes, peeled and chopped
80 g shallots, sliced
100 ml red wine
salt and pepper

PREPARATION

[Serves 4 • Takes 30 minutes]

1. Sauté the porcini mushrooms in the Agnesi extra virgin olive oil for 8 minutes until they are crispy, then add the thyme leaves, potatoes and shallots and sauté for a few more minutes.
2. Reduce the heat and add the red wine. Season to taste with salt and pepper. Put on the lid and simmer the sauce for 20 minutes.

TOMATOES, GINGER AND HONEY

Pomodoro e Zenzero

INGREDIENTS

500 g canned whole peeled tomatoes
40 g onions, peeled and chopped
30 g garlic, peeled and chopped
500 ml Agnesi extra virgin olive oil
20 g coriander leaves, shredded
30 ml honey
40 g ginger, sliced
300 ml rice vinegar
salt and pepper

PREPARATION [Serves 4 • Takes 35 minutes]

1. Purée the tomatoes in a blender and pass it through a fine-mesh sieve.
2. Sauté the onions and garlic in the Agnesi extra virgin olive oil until the garlic is lightly browned. Add the coriander leaves and tomato purée and cook for 15 minutes.
3. Cook the honey and ginger over low heat for 7 minutes. Add the rice vinegar and cook until it evaporates.
4. Add this mixture to the tomato sauce, mix well and cook for 10 minutes. Season to taste with salt and pepper.

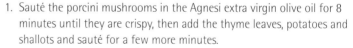

CHICKEN AND SPRING ONION RAGOUT

Pollo e Cipollotti

INGREDIENTS

5 g thyme leaves
10 g parsley, chopped
500 ml Agnesi extra virgin olive oil
300 g chicken breast, diced
10 g plain flour
500 ml dry white wine
100 g spring onion,
   cut each stalk into 4 parts
100 ml warm chicken stock
60 g tomatoes, peeled
salt and pepper

PREPARATION

[Serves 4 • Takes 35 minutes]

1. Preheat the oven at 200 °C.
2. Sauté the thyme leaves and parsley in the Agnesi extra virgin olive oil for a few minutes, then add the chicken and toss well. Add the plain flour and white wine, and cook until the wine has evaporated.
3. Add the spring onion, chicken stock and tomatoes, and season to taste with salt and pepper. Put on the lid, transfer the pan into the oven and let the mixture cook for 25 minutes. Mix well to serve.

MIXED CHEESE FONDUE

Formaggi in Fonduta

INGREDIENTS

400 ml cream
20 g garlic, peeled
50 g fontina cheese, cut into cubes
50 g Taleggio or mozzarella cheese,
   cut into cubes
50 g Gorgonzola cheese,
   cut into cubes
pepper
40 g Parmesan cheese, grated
1 egg yolk

PREPARATION   [Serves 4 • Takes 50 minutes]

1. Combine the cream and garlic in a stainless steel mixing bowl or a heatproof dish and place the bowl in a basin of hot water. Add the cheeses and let the mixture stand for 45 minutes. Mix well with a wooden spatula at regular intervals.
2. Remove the bowl from the hot water and remove the garlic. Season to taste with pepper and add the Parmesan cheese and egg yolk. Mix well to obtain a smooth texture and creamy consistency.

GARLIC, OLIVE OIL AND CHILLI

Aglio, Olio e Peperoncino

INGREDIENTS

80 g garlic, thinly sliced
100 ml Agnesi extra virgin olive oil
40 g red chilli, sliced
50 g parsley, chopped
salt

PREPARATION

[Serves 4 • Takes 15 minutes]

1. Sauté the garlic in the Agnesi extra virgin olive oil over low heat for a few minutes until golden brown.
2. Add the red chilli and parsley and toss well. Season to taste with salt. If the sauce is too spicy, add a little of the water used to cook the pasta or white wine to neutralise it.

MINCED BEEF WITH TOMATOES

Bolognese

INGREDIENTS

40 g carrots, peeled and chopped
40 g onion, peeled and chopped
40 g celery, chopped
20 g garlic, peeled and chopped
50 g soft butter
300 minced beef
50 g bacon, minced
30 g plain flour
500 ml red wine
10 g tomato paste
1 litre warm vegetable stock
salt and pepper

PREPARATION

[Serves 4 • Takes 2 hours]

1. Sauté the carrots, onion, celery and garlic in the butter over low heat for a few minutes.
2. Add the minced beef and bacon, and cook for another 8 minutes.
3. Add the plain flour and mix well. After 5 minutes, add the red wine and cook until the wine has evaporated.
4. Add the tomato paste and vegetable stock. Mix well and season to taste with salt and pepper. Simmer the sauce for 90 minutes or until desired consistency without covering the pot.

BACON WITH CREAM

Carbonara

INGREDIENTS

100 g pancetta (Italian bacon), diced
30 g butter
500 ml dry white wine
600 ml cream
2 egg yolks
50 g Parmesan cheese, grated
10 g crushed black pepper

PREPARATION

[Serves 4 • Takes 15 minutes]

1. Pan-fry the pancetta in the butter until the butter starts to brown. Add the white wine and cook until it evaporates.
2. In a separate pan, combine the cream, egg yolks, Parmesan cheese and black pepper, and cook over medium heat for a few minutes. Mix well to obtain a smooth texture.
3. Add the pancetta to the cream sauce and mix well.

MIXED VEGETABLE RAGOUT
Vegetariana

INGREDIENTS

50 g carrots, peeled and diced
10 g onions, peeled and chopped
100 ml Agnesi extra virgin olive oil
50 g potatoes, peeled and diced
50 g tomatoes, peeled,
   seeds removed and diced
20 g cauliflower,
   cut into florets
100 ml warm vegetable stock
50 g parsley
salt and pepper
50 g zucchini, diced
50 g green peas
30 g broccoli, cut into florets
1 litre salted boiling water
1 litre iced water
5 basil leaves, shredded

PREPARATION

[Serves 4 • Takes 35 minutes]

1. Sauté the carrots and onions in half the Agnesi extra virgin olive oil
   for a few minutes, then add the potatoes, tomatoes, cauliflower, and
   vegetable stock. Cook for 15 minutes.
2. Process the parsley with the remaining olive oil in a blender to
   obtain a smooth purée, then season to taste with salt and pepper.
3. Poach the zucchini, green peas and broccoli in the salted boiling
   water for a few minutes, then strain and refresh in the iced water
   immediately. Strain and add them and the basil to the vegetable
   sauce. Season to taste with salt and pepper, and cook the mixture
   for 5 minutes.
4. Add the parsley purée and mix well.

TOMATOES WITH BASIL
Pomodoro e Basilico

INGREDIENTS

500 g ripe tomatoes
1 litre salted boiling water
40 g onions, peeled and chopped
500 ml Agnesi extra virgin olive oil
20 g basil leaves, shredded
salt and pepper

PREPARATION

[Serves 4 • Takes 30 minutes]

1. Blanch the tomatoes in the
   salted boiling water for 2
   minutes. Peel off the skin, cut
   them into wedges and remove
   the seeds.
2. Sauté the onions in the Agnesi
   extra virgin olive oil for a few
   minutes, then add the basil
   leaves and tomato wedges,
   and cook for 15 minutes.
   Season to taste with salt and
   pepper, and whisk the sauce
   to obtain a smooth texture.

MIX AND MATCH: INVENT YOUR OWN PASTA DISHES

It is easy to improvise and create your own pasta recipes, and with experience you'll develop an intuitive feel of how to match the respective pasta shapes with complementing textures and flavours. The general rule recommends that 'less is more', since limiting the number of ingredients will actually bring out each flavour better.

For healthier sauces, use broths or vegetables as your base, instead of cream and butter. A basic, no-frills dressing can be whipped up with just olive oil, garlic, marinated tomatoes, fresh basil and pepper flakes. Eggplant purée gives your sauces a creamy texture, and it works as well as ricotta cheese. You can also try various spices to liven up existing recipes, particularly for meat sauces: experiment to confirm the exact quantity and blend of spices for each recipe.

Salads Small and light shapes like penne, fusilli, conchigliette are recommended; these mix easily with the other salad ingredients and are unlikely to get tangled up.

Heavy sauces You may pair this with pappardelle, fettuccine or linguine: the flat surface areas allow lots of sauce to adhere easily when you lift your noodles with a fork.

Smooth, light sauces Spaghetti, tagliolini or orecchiette can be easily maneuvered around the plates to pick up the sauces.

Cream sauces These are traditionally paired with fettuccine, spaghetti or smooth penne.

Chunky sauces Meat or vegetable chunks go well with farfalle, fusilli, penne rigate and conchiglioni, which somewhat mimic the size and 'bite' of the ingredients.

Soups Try small pasta like orecchiette, conchiglette or ditalini, which are ideal for giving body to broths and soups.

Baked casseroles These work well with maccheroni, penne rigate, lasagne and fusilli.

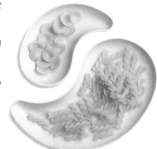